A Brighter Garden

A Brighter Garden

Poetry by Emily Dickinson

Collected by Karen Ackerman

Paintings by Tasha Tudor

Tasha Tudor

Philomel Books

New York

Published by Philomel Books,

a division of The Putnam and Grosset Group.

200 Madison Avenue, New York, NY 10016.

All rights reserved. Published simultaneously in Canada.

Printed in Hong Kong by South China Printing Co. (1988) Ltd.

The text is set in Bembo with Centaur Display.

Book design by Nanette Stevenson.

Library of Congress Cataloging-in-Publication Data

Dickinson, Emily, 1830–1886. A brighter garden.

Summary: An illustrated collection of poems

by the famous nineteenth-century poet.

[1. American poetry]   I. Ackerman, Karen,

II. Tudor, Tasha, ill.   III. Title.

PS1541.A6   1989   811'.4   88-5849

ISBN 0-399-21490-9

First Impression

For Carly and Daniel,
and, with Possibility, for Carol.
K A

These illustrations are dedicated to Miss. Dickinson
with profound respect.
T T

Introduction

". . . *Here* is a little forest,
Whose leaf is ever green;
Here is a brighter garden,
Where not a frost has been;
In its unfading flowers
I hear the bright bee hum;
Prithee, my brother,
Into *my* garden come!"

When Emily Dickinson wrote this poem in 1851, she was not quite twenty years old and was living with her family in the small town of Amherst, Massachusetts.

During the next twenty years, she would write one thousand, seven hundred and seventy-five poems. Sitting alone in the quiet of her room, Emily began writing poetry unlike any other verse written before. She had doubts that her poems would ever be published, and she certainly had little hope that her words would be read by generations to follow.

Yet her poems survive, and one of the reasons that her poetry is still read and enjoyed more than one hundred years after her death is the completely original way in which she wrote about ordinary things.

One of her favorite subjects was the special connection between Nature and human beings. These poems show her extraordinary understanding of how people, plants, and animals all share Nature's cycle of life in Spring (birth), Summer (youth), Autumn (adulthood), and Winter (growing old).

I first read the poetry of Emily Dickinson when I was a high school student. Two decades later, her words still come to mind when I take a walk on a spring day, rake leaves in the yard in the fall, snip roses from the garden in summer, or simply look out of my kitchen window at new-fallen snow on a winter afternoon.

I believe, with all of my heart, that I recall her poetry at these moments because Emily Dickinson intended to touch the child within us all through her poems, and because she believed, as I do, that the child who sees each season of the year as a new and uncomplicated miracle never really grows old.

With great pleasure and honor, I present to young readers these selections from Emily Dickinson's timeless poetry. It is my sincere hope that each of you will find, as I have, happiness in her "brighter garden."

Karen Ackerman

Summer

From Cocoon forth a Butterfly
As Lady from her Door
Emerged—a Summer Afternoon—
Repairing Everywhere—

Without Design—that I could trace
Except to stray abroad
On Miscellaneous Enterprise
The Clovers—understood—

. . .

Till Sundown crept—a steady Tide—
And Men that made the Hay—
And Afternoon—and Butterfly—
Extinguished—in the Sea—

I'm Nobody! Who are you?
Are you—Nobody—Too?
Then there's a pair of us!
Don't tell! they'd advertise—you know!

How dreary—to be—Somebody!
How public—like a Frog—
To tell one's name—the livelong June—
To an admiring Bog!

The Bee is not afraid of me.
I know the Butterfly.
The pretty people in the Woods
Receive me cordially—

The Brooks laugh louder when I come—
The Breezes madder play;
Wherefore mine eye thy silver mists,
Wherefore, Oh Summer's Day?

We should not mind so small a flower—
Except it quiet bring
Our little garden that we lost
Back to the Lawn again.

So spicy her Carnations nod—
So drunken, reel her Bees—
So silver steal a hundred flutes
From out a hundred trees—

That whoso sees this little flower
By faith may clear behold
The Bobolinks around the throne
And Dandelions gold.

To make a prairie it takes a clover and one bee,
One clover, and a bee,
And revery.
The revery alone will do
If bees are few.

The Moon was but a Chin of Gold
A Night or two ago—
And now she turns Her perfect Face
Upon the World below—

Her Forehead is of Amplest Blonde—
Her Cheek—a Beryl hewn—
Her Eye unto the Summer Dew
The likest I have known—

Autumn

I'll tell you how the Sun rose—
A Ribbon at a time—
The Steeples swam in Amethyst—
The news, like Squirrels, ran—

The Clouds their Backs together laid
The North begun to push
The Forests galloped till they fell
The Lightning playcd like mice

The morns are meeker than they were—
The nuts are getting brown—
The berry's cheek is plumper—
The Rose is out of town.

The Maple wears a gayer scarf—
The field a scarlet gown—
Lest I should be old fashioned
I'll put a trinket on.

Frequently the woods are pink—
Frequently are brown.
Frequently the hills undress
Behind my native town.

Before the ice is in the pools —
Before the skaters go,
Or any cheek at nightfall
Is tarnished by the snow —

Before the fields have finished,
Before the Christmas tree,
Wonder upon wonder
Will arrive to me!

. . .

That which sings so — speaks so —
When there's no one here —
Will the frock I wept in
Answer me to wear?

God made a little Gentian—
It tried—to be a Rose—
And failed—and all the Summer laughed—
But just before the Snows

There rose a Purple Creature—
That ravished all the Hill—
And Summer hid her Forehead—
And Mockery—was still—

Winter

The Sky is low—the Clouds are mean.
A Travelling Flake of Snow
Across a Barn or through a Rut
Debates if it will go—

A Narrow Wind complains all Day
How some one treated him
Nature, like Us is sometimes caught
Without her Diadem.

It sifts from Leaden Sieves—
It powders all the Wood.
It fills with Alabaster Wool
The Wrinkles of the Road—

It makes an Even Face
Of Mountain, and of Plain—
Unbroken Forehead from the East
Unto the East again—

It reaches to the Fence—
It wraps it Rail by Rail
Till it is lost in Fleeces—
It deals Celestial Vail

. . .

It Ruffles Wrists of Posts
As Ankles of a Queen—
Then stills its Artisans—like Ghosts—
Denying they have been—

Like Brooms of Steel
The Snow and Wind
Had swept the Winter Street—

These are the days that Reindeer love
And pranks the Northern Star—
This is the Sun's objective,
And Finland of the Year.

Forever honored be the Tree
Whose Apple Winterworn
Enticed to Breakfast from the Sky
Two Gabriels Yestermorn.

Spring

Dear March—Come in—
How glad I am—
I hoped for you before—
Put down your Hat—
You must have walked—
How out of Breath you are—
Dear March, how are you, and the Rest—
Did you leave Nature well—
Oh March, Come right up stairs with me—
I have so much to tell—

A Light exists in Spring
Not present on the Year
At any other period—
When March is scarcely here

. . .

It waits upon the Lawn,
It shows the furthest Tree
Upon the furthest Slope you know
It almost speaks to you.

The saddest noise, the sweetest noise,
   The maddest noise that grows, —
The birds, they make it in the spring,
   At night's delicious close.

The Dandelion's pallid tube
Astonishes the Grass,
And Winter instantly becomes
An infinite Alas—

Where Ships of Purple—gently toss—
On Seas of Daffodil—
Fantastic Sailors—mingle—
And then—the Wharf is still!

Index of First Lines

———

♦ Indicates excerpt. Anthologist Karen Ackerman selected and excerpted Ms. Dickinson's poems particularly with children in mind. Note: As Emily Dickinson did not entitle her poems, they are frequently identified by their first lines. Ms. Dickinson's complete poems were originally compiled and organized by Thomas H. Johnson for the Belknap Press of Harvard University Press and published in three volumes in 1955.

About Tasha Tudor

Born in Boston in 1915, Tasha Tudor spent part of her childhood in rural Connecticut and quickly discovered her love of the New England countryside and its simple life. Her mother, Rosamond Tudor, was a skilled portrait artist, and her father, William Starling Burgess, was a brilliant and innovative naval architect and pioneer in early aviation, as well as a talented storyteller. Both parents encouraged and inspired their daughter to pursue her love of painting, and at the age of twenty-three she published her first book, *Pumpkin Moonshine.*

Since then she has continued to live and work in the old-fashioned and rustic style that first attracted her as a child. The eighteenth-century New Hampshire farmhouse in which her four children were raised provided many of the scenes and much of the inspiration for her books. Both her children and grandchildren have served as models for Ms. Tudor's illustrations, dressing up in vintage costumes from the attic. Her prized Welsh corgis have had a book, *Corgiville Fair,* devoted to them.

Ms. Tudor has long felt a kinship with Emily Dickinson, sharing her love and sensitivity for the ever-changing seasons and the natural world around her. It has been a particular delight for Ms. Tudor to interpret the poetry that she has loved and appreciated since she was a child.